NATURE'S CYCLES

SEED, SPROUT, FRUIT

An Apple Tree Life Cycle

BY SHANNON KNUDSEN

ILLUSTRATED BY SIMON SMITH

Raintree

www.raintreepublishers.co.uk
Visit our website to find out
more information about
Raintree books.

To order:
☎ Phone 0845 6044371
🖷 Fax +44 (0) 1865 312263
🖳 Email myorders@raintreepublishers.co.uk

Customers from outside the UK please telephone +44 1865 312262

Raintree is an imprint of Capstone
Global Library Limited,
a company incorporated in England
and Wales having its
registered office at 7 Pilgrim Street,
London, EC4V 6LB
– Registered company number:
6695582

Text © Capstone Global Library
Limited 2012
First published in 2012
The moral rights of the proprietor
have been asserted.

Designed by Lori Bye and
Victoria Allen
Art Director Nathan Gassman
Production by Victoria Fitzgerald
Originated by Capstone Global
Library Ltd.
Printed and bound in China by
Leo Paper Products Ltd.

ISBN 978 1 406 23004 8
15 14 13 12 11
10 9 8 7 6 5 4 3 2 1

**British Library Cataloguing in
Publication Data**
Knudsen, Shannon, 1971-
Seed, sprout, fruit : an apple tree
life cycle. -- (Nature cycles)
1. Apples--Life cycles--Comic
books, strips, etc.--
Juvenile literature.
I. Title II. Series
571.8'2373-dc22

Disclaimer
All the Internet addresses (URLs)
given in this book were valid at the
time of going to press. However,
due to the dynamic nature of the
Internet, some addresses may have
changed, or sites may have changed
or ceased to exist since publication.
While the author and Publishers
regret any inconvenience this may
cause readers, no responsibility for
any such changes can be accepted
by either the author or
the Publishers.

Contents

Start with a seed

Do you like apples?

Crunch!

Mmm!

Slurp!

APPLE SAUCE

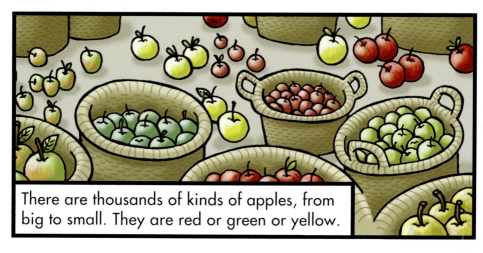

There are thousands of kinds of apples, from big to small. They are red or green or yellow.

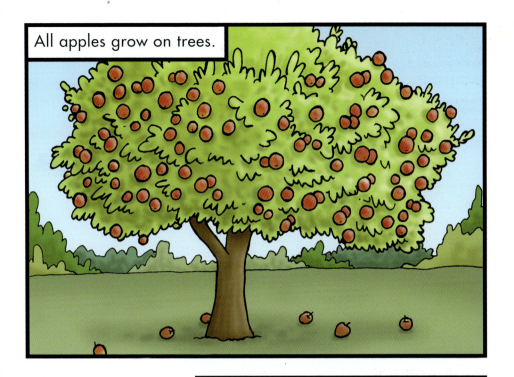

All apples grow on trees.

During its life, an apple tree goes through a series of changes, or cycle.

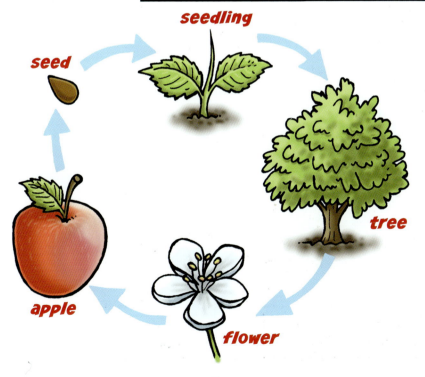

seedling

seed

tree

apple

flower

5

Apple trees start with a seed in the soil.

Its roots push into the soil. They take in water and minerals.

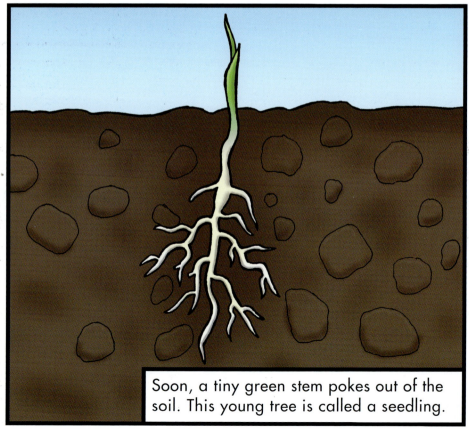

Soon, a tiny green stem pokes out of the soil. This young tree is called a seedling.

As the seedling grows, it sprouts leaves. Chlorophyll in leaves makes them green.

Chlorophyll also helps the tree make food. The leaves take in carbon dioxide (CO_2) gas and energy from sunlight.

Using chlorophyll and water, the tree makes sugar. Sugar gives the seedling energy to grow.

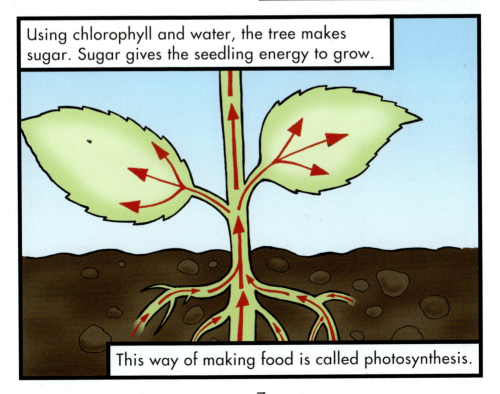

This way of making food is called photosynthesis.

At first, seedlings are tender. Animals may eat them.

Insects may eat the leaves.

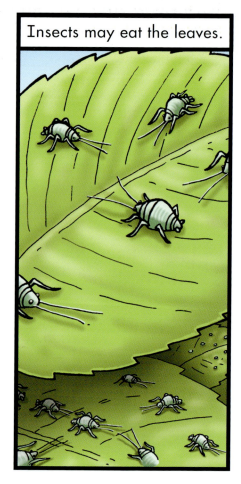

At any time in the life cycle, lack of rain could kill a tree.

Diseases could also kill the apple tree at any age.

Seedlings that live grow tall. Their trunks thicken. More and more branches sprout.

In autumn the weather turns cool. Days get shorter.

With less sunlight, leaves lose their chlorophyll. They change colour.

Then they drift to the ground.

10

Winter comes. The apple tree is bare, but it's still alive. It is dormant.

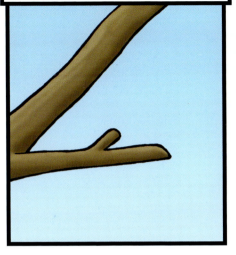

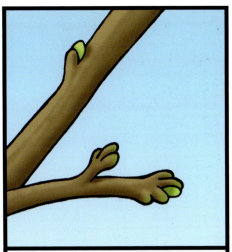

In spring, the little tree grows buds. New leaves open from the buds.

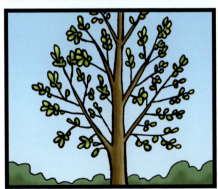

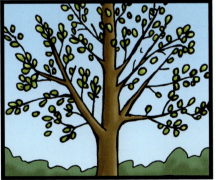

The tree spends four to seven years passing through the seasons, growing bigger and stronger.

Flower power

After five to seven years, the tree is an adult. It is springtime of this tree's fifth year. Buds appear on its branches.

Like before, the buds open into leaves. But something new happens, too.

Flower buds appear in the centre of the leaf clusters.

Soon the tree is covered with blossom.

An apple tree's flowers have an important job. They make a sweet liquid called nectar.

Nectar is food for bees.

Flowers also make tiny yellow grains called pollen.

Pollen grains stick to the bees as they sip the nectar.

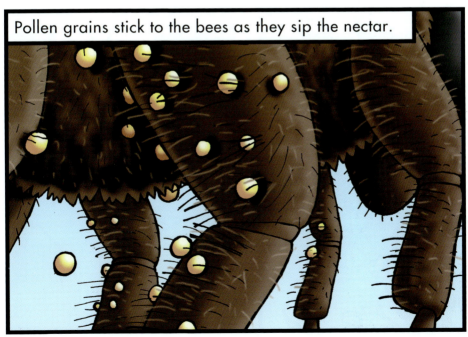

Healthy apples ripen over the summer. In autumn people pick apples to eat.

Some apples fall to the ground. They make tasty food for wandering animals.

Animals drop the apple seeds in new places when they poo. The seeds mix in the soil.

Winter comes. Tiny seeds lie frozen in the soil. What will happen when spring comes?

In spring, the soil thaws. A seedling sprouts.

And the apple tree life cycle begins again.

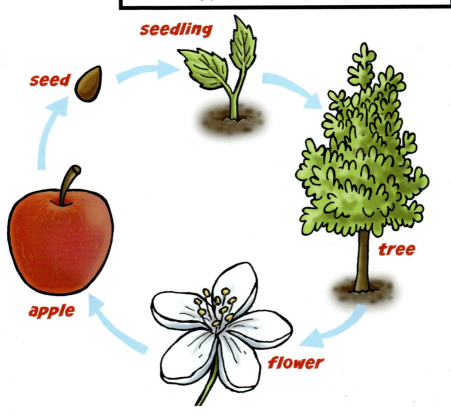

seed

seedling

tree

flower

apple

Index